The Story of Huey Long, the Louisiana Kingfish

REINHARD H. LUTHIN

Text originally published in 1954 as a section of *American Demagogues: Twentieth Century*, by Reinhard H. Luthin
Original copyright 1954 The Beacon Press (not renewed)

Republished 2020 by A. J. Cornell Publications

ISBN: 978-1660196968

I

Huey Long was born in a log house at Winnfield, the parish seat of Winn Parish, in north central Louisiana, on August 30, 1893. "Huey was, I think, the eighth," Huey Long Sr. told an interviewer at the age of eighty-one. "I'd have to see—seven, eight, nine, ten—yes, Huey was the eighth child." Huey Jr. maintained that his blood was highly mixed—English, Dutch, Welsh, Scotch, and French—though some critics insisted that the last claim was only an appeal to the French-descended voters of southern Louisiana.

In contrast to Cajun and Roman Catholic southern Louisiana, the hills of the northern parishes were populated predominantly by Anglo-Saxon Protestants—Holy Rollers and hard-shelled Baptists, among whom the Longs were numbered. The Bible was the only volume, aside from the Sears-Roebuck catalogue, in the average home of Winn Parish. Young Huey memorized whole passages from the New Testament. "In the country where I came from," he declared later, "most every summer we held a religious revival called a camp meeting. People came from miles around, bringing their dinner baskets. Preaching lasted all day, with dinner on the table at noon." Later, Long the demagogue was to exploit the emotional techniques he had learned from the evangelists.

When he grew up and was looking for votes, Long recalled that he had been an overworked farm boy, "rising before the sun" and "toiling until dark." In campaign literature he claimed to have saved money for his education out of his daily pittance of thirty-five cents. His brother, however, maintained that the family was prosperous enough to send several of the boys to college. "Huey never had to work a day in the fields only as he wanted to in his life," his father said.

At Winnfield High School, elocution became Huey's favorite subject. At sixteen he left home and peddled books, soap, groceries, furniture, clothing, and starch from door to door. He tramped the northern parishes selling medicine and a vegetable shortening lard substitute. He trekked from kitchen to kitchen, introducing himself to housewives and persuading them to abandon "cow butter" and "hog lard" for his product. He conducted baking contests among the women and handed out the prizes.

Long could out-talk competitors and customers alike. He came to know the hill-folk of the upper parishes as no Louisiana politician ever had. He retained memories of squalid living conditions, poor roads, inadequate schools, and a host of popular prejudices. He compiled mailing lists of his customers, which he was to use in later years for distributing campaign pamphlets.

In 1912 Long attended the University of Oklahoma. During his brief stay at the university in Norman, he organized a students' club to promote the Democratic presidential ambitions of Speaker of Congress Champ Clark of Missouri. But when his funds ran out, he left college and went back as drummer on the Louisiana road.

During his vegetable shortening days, Long had awarded a prize for the best "bride loaf cake" to a young lady of Shreveport, Miss Rose McConnell. Now he returned to the city and married her. Some months later, at his wife's urging, he borrowed $400 and enrolled at Tulane University in New Orleans as a special law student.

When Long's loan was exhausted after seven months, he asked Chief Justice Frank A. Monroe of the Louisiana Supreme Court for permission to take an examination for admission to the bar. The Chief Justice referred him to the bar examination committee, and Long sought each member out and urged his case. After they granted his request, he passed the special examination and was sworn in as a member of the Louisiana bar on May 15, 1915. Not yet twenty-two years old, the redheaded youth from the red hills had mastered a three-year law course in less than one year.

When the United States declared war on Germany in 1917, Long claimed exemption from the draft because he was married and a notary public—hence a "state official"! Instead of serving in the army, he sold patent medicines in Baton Rouge.

II

"The State was run by an oligarchy of a few families," Huey Long once told a writer who inquired about Louisiana conditions before he rose to power. "All of them lived off the people.... The political families worked in with the big corporations, and their members had fancy jobs with the corporations ruling the state."

Long's diagnosis was essentially correct. The bulk of the Pelican State's wealth and political power rested in a few hands. The well-to-do planters and corporations worked hand-in-glove with the leaders of an entrenched political machine in New Orleans, often referred to as the "Tammany Hall of the South." With the aid of this machine, Standard Oil Company and public utility corporations, controlled by northeastern financial interests, had staked out huge claims on the state's resources in the early 20th century.

In Winn Parish, hill people grubbed out a most modest living working for nearby sawmills, or grew cotton on harsh marginal land, with yearly incomes sometimes less than $250. Poverty and illiteracy had always cursed Louisiana. Discontent was apparent in the 1890s, when Populism engulfed Winn, and again in 1908, when a visit by the Socialist presidential candidate, Eugene V. Debs, to Winnfield resulted in the election of half of the police jurors and school trustees on the Socialist ticket. The century-old hatred of the hill people for the plantation owners and for the new hierarchy of business and capital centering in New Orleans, was once explosively expressed by Long's aged father. "There wants to be a revolution, I tell you," insisted the senior Long. "I seen this domination of capital, seen it for seventy years. What do these rich folks care for the poor man? . . . Maybe you're surprised to hear talk like that. Well, it was just such talk that my boy was raised under and that I was raised under." The "poor whites" felt no devotion to the aristocratic traditions of the pre–Civil War era.

Before Huey Long's rise to power, those who controlled Louisiana politics had done little if anything about the low rate of literacy and the maldistribution of wealth. No Moses—such as Jim Vardaman in Mississippi, Jeff Davis in Arkansas, Tom Watson in Georgia, or Ben Tillman in South Carolina—had appeared in Louisiana to lead the "poor white" crusade.

Louisiana tradition has it that Long read and was considerably influenced by Samuel G. Blythe's satirical novel of a demagogue who gained a United States seat. *The Fakers,* published in 1914, emphasized the campaign tactics of a spellbinding speaker with a bag of tricks, the most effective of which was a verbal assault on the Standard Oil Company. Perhaps the book gave Long an appreciation of histrionics and showmanship as weapons of political warfare. At least

Huey is quoted by one Louisiana student as saying of Blythe: "The fellow that put those views and promises in the mouth of a political candidate thought he was writing something funny; and he was, at that. But he was also writing something of immense value to the man who wants to get somewhere in politics. The people want that kind of stuff. They eat it up. Why not give it to them?"

Long was also influenced by his association with State Senator H. J. Harper. Harper had written a pamphlet in 1918 opposing American participation in the war and calling for conscription of money as well as men. Indicted under the Federal Espionage Act, Harper retained Long as counsel. Long defended him in words that revealed his study of Harper's volume: "War should be supported by a conscription of war profits and certain amounts of swollen fortunes, as well as conscription of men, or the country will face financial slavery. Ten percent of the people own seventy percent of the wealth."

Long continued his battle against entrenched wealth that year when he campaigned for the railroad commissionership of North Louisiana in the Democratic primary. He harangued about the "Wall Street money devil" and told one *New Orleans Item* reporter that between 1890 and 1910 "the wealth of the nation trebled, yet the masses owned less in 1910 than in 1890."

During the campaign, Long moved to Shreveport and established headquarters at his father-in-law's house. The newspapers ignored his candidacy, but his wife, in-laws, and friends mailed out letters and leaflets to the rural folk. Establishing a pattern he was to follow in future elections, Long loaded his second-hand automobile with posters and chugged through the northern parishes along the same route he had followed as a drummer. He joined the local farmers in a dish of "pot-likker," made from boiled greens and turnips. He talked to them about plows and politics, crops and credit.

Before Primary Day, the real election in Democratic "one-party" Louisiana, Long's funds ran out. Oscar K. ("O.K.") Allen, a Winnfield storekeeper who had been one of his first clients, signed a $500 note for him at the bank, enabling him to continue his fight. Long triumphed in the primary.

Soon after his election, the new railroad commissioner opened a law office in Shreveport. He built up a reputation as a champion of the common man through his hostility to large corporations, particularly Standard Oil and the public utilities. Several years later he explained to an audience: "As a country yap I put $1,050 in oil stock. The company made a strike, and I was advised to hold on, and I did hold on. Then the big companies, led by the Standard Oil [which owned the pipeline monopoly] issued notices that they would take no more oil from the independent producers and my oil stock wasn't worth forty cents, while oil went to waste. Do you think I can forget that? Do you blame me for fighting the Standard

Oil?"

The only corporations with which most hill people had ever had contact were the sawmills, which bought their timber at "starvation" prices. Most of them could not afford a telephone. Commissioner Long succeeded in having Standard Oil's pipelines declared "common carriers" and in forcing the Cumberland Telephone and Telegraph Company to reduce its rates. He made the Railroad and Public Service Commission the state's most active executive body. The hillbillies spoke of Long affectionately as "that young feller who is fightin' them thievin' millionaires for the benefit of the pore people." When he came up for renomination in the 1924 Democratic primary, he won by a plurality of five to one.

The commissioner engaged in lucrative law practice at Shreveport even while he attended to his official duties. Long might howl against the big corporations on the hustings, but he accepted legal retainers from some of them. "When the millionaires and corporations of Louisiana fell out with each other," he explained in his book, *Every Man a King,* "I was able to accept highly remunerative employment from one of the powerful to fight several others which were even more powerful. Then I made some big fees with which I built a modern home in the best residential section of the City of Shreveport at a cost of $40,000."

III

Commissioner Long worked tirelessly to make himself political chieftain of North Louisiana. His eyes even turned toward the Governor's Mansion in Baton Rouge. Soon he was campaigning actively for at least one candidate in every state campaign.

He electioneered for John M. Parker in the Democratic gubernatorial primary of 1920. "Because of our lack of newspaper support in some sections," he maintained later, "I had thousands of circulars printed for distribution. I took the stump for a period of approximately seventy days and went places where no other campaign orator had ever reached, traveling at times by horseback to fill appointments." Long reminded voters of his services as railroad commissioner; he flooded them with circulars about his crusade against entrenched wealth and the insidious New Orleans political ring. At crossroads and creek forks in the northern parishes, Long lauded Parker's stand in favor of making pipelines common carriers—a thrust at Standard Oil. Parker won the primary, and Long insisted that it was his doing. In that era, before the advent of radio and electrical sound-amplifiers, a candidate's effectiveness was usually proportional to the lustiness of his voice at open-air rallies. Long's lungs were strong.

Long perfected his oratorical technique in these campaigns. He spoke in terms of "we": "We are a-goin' ter do this—we done that." He eschewed polysyllabic words; he exaggerated his "hillbilly" accent; he reveled in the idioms of his native hills. "I am an ignorant man," he later told the United States Senate. "I have had no college education. I have not even had a high school education. . . . I have one language. Ignorant as it is, it is the universal language within the sphere in which I operate. Its simplicity gains pardon for my lack of letters and education." Long's apologies were somewhat disingenuous. His formal education had been spotty, of course, but his ignorance was a pose. He was an able lawyer. Once when he was drunk, he uttered a franker appraisal of his own abilities. "There may be smarter guys than Huey Long," he said, "but they ain't in Louisiana."

Soon after the election, Long broke with the new governor, nominally because Parker was reluctant to levy higher taxes on Standard Oil. On August 30, 1923, his thirtieth birthday, Long announced his own candidacy for the governorship. The campaign began at once.

Some opposition candidates might offer money for votes, Long predicted to his audiences. "So take the money—and then vote for me." He cited his teachers as Abraham Lincoln, Andrew Jackson, and Almighty God. He assailed Governor Parker as "a damnable demagogue." He charged the *New Orleans Item* and the *Times-Picayune* with being journals of Wall Street.

Long personally placarded the back roads and cow-paths with his posters and pictures, remembering the huckstering tricks of his drummer days. "I adopted the art of driving my automobile close to the tall trees," he explained. "From the top I reached with a long hammer as far as possible, to hang my campaign posters beyond the reach of any opponent's hand." Meanwhile, Mrs. Long mailed simply worded, hard-hitting circulars to homes in the northern hills and the southern fishing and shrimp villages—homes into which newspapers rarely entered.

A heavy rain fell on Primary Day, January 15, 1924. Long's rural followers were kept at home. A second cause of his defeat lay in his inability to attract votes in the French parishes.

The ambitious railroad commissioner soon found opportunity to appeal to Catholic Creoles and Cajuns of southern Louisiana. In 1926 United States Senator Edwin S. Broussard came up for reelection. Long set out to sell Broussard—a French Creole Catholic, an advocate of a protective tariff on sugar, and "as wet as Lake Pontchartrain" on the prohibition question—to his Anglo-Saxon Protestant, low-tariff, "dry" followers in northern Louisiana. He stumped the state, told the Creoles that French blood flowed in his own veins, and referred to Broussard as "Couzain Ed." He assured his own disciples of his complete loyalty to the senator. Broussard squeaked through the primary with a 4,000-vote margin. "My disinclination to enter a second race for Governor," Long declared, "soon melted away."

Opposing Long in the gubernatorial primary of

1928 was Congressman Riley Wilson, candidate of the New Orleans "Old Regular" machine, which controlled much of the state through an alliance with the rural courthouse cliques. Long ridiculed Wilson as a "babe," although Wilson was twenty-two years older than himself and had already served seven terms in Congress. Governor O. H. Simpson also filed in the primary.

Long's irrelevant and crudely humorous talk amused his followers. "Most people would rather laugh than weep," he told one correspondent. "When I'm making a political speech, I like to cut around the opposition with a joke." He could make his listeners cry as well as laugh, and he made them weep for more roads and better schools.

Long provided his campaign with a slogan: "Every Man a King but No Man Wears a Crown." Long said he borrowed the vote-catching words from that perennial Democratic-Populist seeker after the presidency, William Jennings Bryan. In a speech on "Imperialism," delivered in the campaign of 1900, the Great Commoner spoke of a "republic in which every citizen is a sovereign, but in which no one cares or dares to wear a crown." Henceforth, "Every Man a King" was to be Long's battle cry.

Long's candidacy was considerably strengthened by the colorless mediocrity of his opponents. And the heavens on Primary Day, 1928, were kind to Long. The sun beamed on his followers as they trekked to the polls. Although he ran third to Wilson and Simpson in New Orleans, he piled up a lead of 40,000 over Wilson in the state. He carried fifty-six of the sixty-four parishes. A few days later Governor Simpson declared for Long, rather than join forces with Wilson in a "run-off" primary. Later Long gave Simpson a state job. Wilson, viewing his chances as hopeless, declined to enter a second primary.

Louisianians expected an unusual gubernatorial term. But they were unprepared for what was to come.

IV

Before he took the oath as governor, Long asked Governor Simpson to begin operation of toll-free ferries in competition with toll bridges across Lake Pontchartrain. Simpson obeyed. Opportunists galore were anxious to clamber aboard Long's bandwagon. He noted gleefully: "No music ever sounded so refreshing as the whines and groans of the pie-eating politicians."

On May 14, 1928, one week before Long's inauguration, the state legislature assembled. An agreement between the forces of Long and Simpson enabled the Long choices, John B. Fournet and Philip H. Gilbert, to be chosen Speaker of the House and President Pro Tempore of the Senate, respectively. Long supervised all legislative committee appointments.

Governor Long's two main objectives were to launch his legislative program and to secure patronage by gaining control of the state's administrative boards. He broke precedent by invading the floor of both houses to line up supporters for his program. With the aid of the Simpsonites, he mustered a majority on almost all occasions. He railroaded bills through the legislature providing for increased taxes on gas and other commodities to raise money for public schools, distribution of free textbooks, construction of bridges and eleemosynary [charitable] institutions, and improvement of roads and highways. He "persuaded" the lawmakers to authorize a $15,000,000 bond issue for the improvement of Lake Pontchartrain at New Orleans.

Long seized control of the state patronage. As chairman of the contract-letting highway commission, he chose his old friend, O.K. Allen of Winnfield. The Governor demanded resignations from public officers whose jobs he controlled and launched schemes to oust others. One "Long law" supplanted the nine-member Orleans Parish Levee Board with a five-member group to be appointed by the governor. Another ended the term of Dr. Oscar Dowling, president of the state Board of Health. His place was given to Dr. Joseph A. O'Hara, a Long satellite. The Governor, in his autobiography, referred to his patronage bills as "legislation needed to strengthen the hand of the administration."

Among Long's constructive achievements during the early months of his regime were the provision of free textbooks, school bus service, and new school buildings; and the construction of new roads throughout the state's muddy terrain. All served to increase his popularity. Yet every legislative proposal, every appointment to office, every public act, was designed to create a loyal and effective machine of which he would be lord. In June 1928, when he entered a controversy with the Public Service Corporation to force it to bring in natural gas to New Orleans at a certain rate, he told the utility managers: "A deck has 52 cards and in Baton Rouge I hold all 52 of them and can shuffle and deal as I please. I can have bills passed or I can kill them. I'll give you until Saturday to decide." They decided to agree with the Governor.

His Excellency's ambitious building program and the job-heavy machine were costly. He needed new taxes. In mid-March, 1929, he called a special session of the legislature to meet objections raised by the United States Supreme Court to certain laws he had sponsored and to make provision for more taxes, particularly an occupational license tax of five cents a barrel on the refining of oil.

The Standard Oil Company threatened to refuse to pay the additional tax. It would close its refinery at Baton Rouge. Soon Standard enlisted support from other companies. Suddenly the Governor abandoned the short session of the legislature and issued a supplemental call for an eighteen-day session. At that session Standard joined hands with other anti-Long elements. When the House met on March 25— sometimes called "Bloody Monday"— one anti-Long member demanded an investigation of charges that Long had hired a gunman to assassinate an anti-Long member, J. Y. Sanders Jr. Longites and anti-Longites among the legislators engaged in fisticuffs in a near riot. Two days later impeachment charges were drawn against the Governor.

In his private chambers Long nervously stalked about the room; his bodyguards shielded him from all visitors except his henchmen. When his opponents held a huge meeting to give support to the impeachment move, Highway Chairman Allen frantically suggested a conclave of pro-Long citizens in Baton Rouge. Allen advised him: "Get those circulars going. Get up a mass meeting! Get it up quick!" Long's crony, Robert Maestri, wealthy New Orleans businessman, inquired how soon money would be needed with which to turn out the printed calls-to-arms. Long snapped: "Just as soon as a printing office can turn out circulars and the government can sell stamps." Maestri made huge funds available. Tens of thousands of circulars were soon speeded to central distributing points by highway policemen and state officers.

From the country parishes, Long loyalists, some in overalls, flocked into Baton Rouge to demonstrate their confidence. The charges against their beloved Huey were pure lies, trumped up by conniving corporations because he was the "pore" man's friend. The Governor himself recalled with relish: "The city was swamped. Even the streets could hardly hold the crowds. . . . Hurriedly as the meeting was called, it was a panic, and very few of the laborers and farmers had taken time to change their working clothes to come to the capital." Long's lieutenant and chief counsel, John H. Overton, addressed the mob through a loudspeaker: "As I see him there now, with his rapier flashing, fencing off the enemies to the left, to the front and to the right, when this smoke of battle shall have cleared, as in the beginning, I will be standing or lying by the side of Huey P. Long." In the evening the Governor spoke for two hours. He roared: "The man who dares to undertake the destruction of these entrenched forces and the taxation of the powerful interests of this State, faces an impeachment." Near midnight he closed dramatically with the poem: "I am the Captain of My Soul."

The distribution of pro-Long circulars, such as "The Standard Oil Company vs. Huey P. Long," continued feverishly. While the impeachment proceedings were being concluded by the lower house for presentation to the state senate, which would sit as a court, the Governor toured the state. "God give me the voice and weather for open meetings," he implored, "and the people will know my side."

Back in Baton Rouge, Long summoned fifteen of the state senators. By cajolery, promises of patronage, and threats of opposition when they came up for renomination, he persuaded the fifteen to sign a "round robin" manifesto, their signatures arranged in circular form so as to disguise the order of signing. In the "round robin" they served notice on their senatorial colleagues that they would not vote for a guilty verdict against the Governor. Since twenty-six senators were required to convict, the impeachers faced certain defeat and agreed to the adjournment of the senate court. Long's trial ended before it started.

As the senate court was adjourning, jubilant officeholders swarmed about Long, like flies around drying Louisiana shrimp. He scrawled his name for autograph-seekers: "Governor of Louisiana, By the Grace of the People."

V

The "Famous Fifteen" senators who had signed the "round robin" received rich business and political plums from the grateful Governor. With the United States Senate as his goal, Long went on to increase his power and strengthen his political machine.

By 1930 Long had moved his law office from Shreveport to New Orleans. He formed the Louisiana Democratic Association (LDA), a machine fueled by state and local patronage—with ward leaders, precinct captains, and all the trappings and artifices of the rival New Orleans "Old Regulars." Long had Robert Maestri made head of the LDA in the Crescent City, and his friend, Dr. Joseph A. O'Hara, chosen state president. Long considered, so he said, the patronage part of party power undesirable but necessary. Once he exploded: "If I didn't have a good organization, they could get back in power and suppress Huey P.

Long and what he's done for Loozyana.... If I had my way I wouldn't have a ward leader in Loozyana. I'd get up a program and go to the people naked, without organization, and say, 'Here's what I'll do for you if you put me in.' But if I did that, the old gang would have all the ward leaders on their side."

Long kept his organization amply supplied with money. Some corporations opened their purses. Entrepreneurs who received contracts from the state and parish governments realized that they would receive little consideration unless they "put it on the line." The chief of the Enforcement Bureau of the United States Treasury Department, Elmer L. Irey, whose men investigated Long and his lieutenants for income-tax evasion on the graft money they collected, described the situation in his reminiscences, *The Tax-Dodgers:* "The people paid for their books and bridges and roads, and paid and paid and paid. The corporation 'high muckety-mucks' paid too, but they quickly learned that Huey could be shown the unfairness of overly high taxes with arguments based on cash." As for the Governor, "He took plenty and he took it for Huey Pierce Long, which made him a tool of the vested interests he fought so vigorously." Long's loyal followers rationalized the graft, one declaring: "Well, all of 'em before him got it without givin' us nothin'. He's given us some roads so it don't matter if he does steal a little. I would get it if I was in his place."

Long's power was based not only on patronage

and careful organization but also on his vivid personality, his demagogic promises, and his crowd-swaying oratory. Long's endorsement of a candidate was usually sufficient, outside of New Orleans and perhaps Shreveport, to guarantee victory in a Democratic primary. He held the devotion of the masses.

When an official pointed out that contracts should be awarded by the highway commission and not by the Governor, Long answered that he was "the Kingfish of the Lodge," taking the sobriquet from a radio character, "the Kingfish of the Mystic Knights of the Sea," who appeared on the popular *Amos 'n' Andy* program. Long explained: "We used to listen to them blackface fellows on the radio, and somehow or other I got to calling one of my gang 'Brother Crawford' and he took to calling me Kingfish. I took it up myself."

Since the city newspapers and numerous rural weeklies were largely opposed to him—Long called them "the lyin' press"—he started his own journalistic mouthpiece. On March 27, 1930, the first issue of the weekly *Louisiana Progress* appeared. The paper was organized by Colonel James E. Edmonds, a former managing editor of the *Times-Picayune*. The editorship was later taken over by a former reporter for the New Orleans States, John Klorer Jr. Businessmen who were given state contracts were required to advertise in the new weekly. Cartoons by Trist Wood pictorialized Long's opponents as snakes and buzzards. "Trist," as he signed himself, portrayed the principal

New Orleans dailies as grotesque-looking characters who told lies and only lies. The *Progress*'s favorite target was the Constitutional League, a civic group whose announced purpose was to force Long to run the governor's office in accordance with the state and federal constitutions. "Trist" caricatured the league as a balky little mule carrying broken-down politicians. One of the "passengers" was United States Senator Joseph E. Ransdell. On July 17, 1930, the *Progress* announced in a banner headline: "Long Runs for the Senate!"

The Kingfish introduced novel campaign methods into the senatorial race. He hired two gaudy, expensive sound trucks. Crews of advance henchmen whipped up crowds with blaring music. All was in readiness when, flanked by bodyguards and policemen and with a Bible beside him, Long raced into town. He instituted a "babysitter" service at outdoor rallies. Young men were hired to mind fretful infants—and to change diapers, if necessary—so that their sun-bonneted mothers could hear Long. Squads of highway surveyors went to remote country parishes with posts and flags to show where the new roads were to be cut "any day now"; if a native asked that the route be shifted a bit so as to run through his property, he was accommodated. They guffawed as the Governor ridiculed the elderly, goateed Ransdell as "Old Feather Duster."

In collaring "labor" votes Long secured a letter favoring his senatorial candidacy from President William Green of the American Federation of Labor. Since Senator Ransdell was a Catholic and opposed prohibition, Long circulated leaflets in "dry" Protestant North Louisiana posing the question: "Shall rum, Romanism, and ruin rule?" He appealed to big-city voters: "I have a plan that will take the City of New Orleans out of debt in twenty-four hours." But he did not divulge the miraculous formula. To the unemployed he promised the "Long plan": "When it goes into effect there won't be a jobless man in America." But he declined to reveal the cure-all.

Ransdell was helpless before the Governor's parish-to-parish whirlwind campaign. Voters were looking for newer and fresher figures in public life. To them the 72-year-old Ransdell had become a shopworn political type. Long defeated the senator by 40,000 votes.

The efficiency of Long's machine was illustrated by the vote in St. Bernard Parish: Long, 3,979; Ransdell, 9—a majority that makes even the Frank Hague machine of Jersey City look amateurish.

Before Senator-elect Long left for Washington, he spoke to former President Coolidge in New Orleans and inquired if President and Mrs. Hoover were "good housekeepers." The none-too-communicative Coolidge assumed that they were. Long answered: "When I was elected here, I had to tear the mansion down. It started a hell of a row. I don't want to have to tear down the White House."

VI

In January 1932 Huey Long took a special train for Washington, D.C., accompanied by a retinue of aides and hangers-on.

Roaring into the Senate chamber like a Louisiana gulf storm, he strutted up and down the aisles, shaking hands with other senators, slapping them on the back, and announcing: "I'm the Kingfish! Who're you?" Most senators found him offensive. In the weeks that followed, he frequently caused the more dignified members to scurry to cloak rooms, while he put on a one-man show for the gallery crowds and press reporters. Waving his arms, his voice booming, he described America's ills, following it with whatever simple remedy that he had in mind at the moment.

The Senate rule permitting unlimited debate was suited to Long's lung power. For decades the national Upper House had endured "filibusterers" who launched endless speeches, usually on extraneous topics, for the purpose of blocking action on legislation. Never had the body listened to one as spectacular and coarse as Long.

The performance which Long staged in January 1933, when Senator Carter Glass of Virginia introduced a banking bill, became a classic of demagoguery. Ranting against branch banking, he quoted from Isaiah in the Bible: "Woe unto them that join house to house that lay field to field, till there be no place, that they may be placed alone in the midst of the earth!" This passage, he avowed, applied to bankers—and to United States Senators. All that was necessary to put in there, Long instructed, were the words, "banking house to banking house and woe be unto them." He challenged the wealthy classes: "Go to now, ye rich men, weep and howl your miseries that shall come upon you." When Connecticut Senator Hiram Bingham reminded him that he was holding up the appropriation of funds for the needy, Long snapped: "I decline to yield to any senator who has not a good record in behalf of the poor people or the kind of a poor people's record that I have."

Meanwhile, the Senator from Louisiana garnered nationwide publicity for his "Share-Our-Wealth" panacea.

Late in April, Long introduced a resolution calling on the Senate Finance Committee to revise the pending revenue bill so that incomes exceeding $1,000,000 a year and inheritances above $5,000,000 would be confiscated. Senator Joseph T. Robinson of Arkansas, the Democratic leader, opposed it. The Louisianian replied with a scathing attack on Robinson. The Share-Our-Wealth plan, Long asserted, accorded with the Declaration of Independence and the principles of Jefferson, Jackson, and Bryan, whereas Robinson followed the dictates of Herbert Hoover, Bernard Baruch, and Rockefeller. He had the Congressional Record print a list of the Arkansas senator's law clients, including corporations and banks.

Long devoured ever more of the Senate's time. His

filibuster of June 1935, against the Roosevelt administration's proposed extension of the National Recovery Act, lasted over fifteen hours. "I desire to ask," he demanded, "that every Senator be made to stay and listen to me, unless he has himself excused." He bathed his foes in vitriol: "pot-bellied politician," "scoundrel," and "chinch bug," he shouted. He commented on the preservation of eyesight, discoursed on Frederick the Great and Judah P. Benjamin (Jefferson Davis's secretary of state), and he read from Victor Hugo. He enlightened his colleagues: "I will accommodate any senator tonight on any point on which he needs advice." He dictated recipes for fried oysters, Roquefort cheese dressing, and pot-likker. Only one other member in the Senate's history to that time—Senator Robert M. La Follette Sr., of Wisconsin, who filibustered against a currency bill in 1908 for eighteen hours—had exceeded Long's marathon talkfest. He collected more publicity, at a cost to the taxpayers of $5,000 to print his 150,000 words in the *Congressional Record*.

Newspaper editors and reporters marked the Louisiana demagogue as colorful copy. When he insisted that corn pone should be "dunked" and not "crumbled" into pot-likker and had himself photographed dunking, the *Atlanta Constitution* protested that all well-mannered Southerners crumbled. The controversy led reporters to seek out the opinion on that momentous question of Governor Franklin D. Roosevelt of New York, then a candidate for the Democratic presidential nomination. Roosevelt replied that both "dunking" and "crumbling" were excellent ways to consume pot-likker and that he used them both.

VII

The Senator from Louisiana utilized the 1932 elections to increase his influence nationally.

At the Democratic National Convention in Chicago during June 1932, Long thrust himself to the front. Surrounded by his bodyguards, he barged into the hotel room of Edward J. Flynn, Boss of the Bronx, and announced that he was for Roosevelt for the presidential nomination. The delighted Flynn, a Roosevelt leader, assured him that the New York Governor's forces would support Long's Louisiana delegation in preference to a rival one. The Senator appeared before the convention's credentials committee and delivered an unusually reasoned, untheatrical argument as to why his delegation should be seated. The committee, dominated by Roosevelt men, agreed. Once his group was officially seated, Long waltzed cockily into caucus rooms, roared instructions to henchmen, and engaged in verbal tilts with other delegates and newspapermen.

Long played a role in the nomination of Roosevelt for president. During the third ballot, James A. Farley and others of the New York Governor's high command at Chicago grew nervous lest the Arkansas and Mississippi delegations, the majority of whom were for Roosevelt, would abandon the rule that bound all delegates of those states to vote as a unit. The situation alarmed the Roosevelt strategists since Arkansas came early in the alphabetical balloting; should Arkansas waiver in its devotion to FDR, other states might follow. Arkansas was looking to Mississippi for guidance. The Roosevelt managers asked Long to give immediate attention to both delegations. He hastened to comply. He threatened. He cajoled. He shook his fist into the face of Senator Pat Harrison of Mississippi and shouted: "If you break the rule ... I'll go into Mississippi and break you!" Arkansas and Mississippi held fast to Roosevelt on the crucial ballot. Later Flynn declared: "There is no question in my mind but that without Long's work, Roosevelt might not have been nominated."

Long's experience at Chicago made him yearn for more space in the national limelight. As the presidential campaign got under way, the ambitious Louisianian demanded that Democratic National Chairman James A. Farley arrange for a special train in which he could visit every state in the union, speaking for Roosevelt and promising immediate cash payment of the veterans' bonus. The cost of such a stunt and the fear that Roosevelt might be overshadowed made Farley frown. Long angrily banged his fist on the National Chairman's desk. Finally Farley mapped out for him a speaking tour that would take him only into states believed already lost or so firmly committed to Roosevelt that nothing he did could harm the Democratic ticket. A few weeks after the rabble-rousing Louisianian and his Bible took to the hustings for FDR, Farley's eyes were opened. "I don't hesitate to say," he admitted in reminiscence, "that we underrated Long's ability to grip the masses with his peculiar brand of public speaking, which was a curious hodgepodge of buffoonery and demagogic strutting, cleverly bundled with a lot of shrewd common sense and an evangelical fervor in discussing the plight of the underprivileged. He put on a great show and everywhere he went, we got the most glowing reports of what he had accomplished for the Democratic cause. . . . We never again underrated him."

Long took enough time out from his national politicking to help Mrs. Hattie Caraway of Arkansas in her campaign for election to a full term in the United States Senate. Mrs. Caraway had been appointed to fill her late husband's unexpired Senate term. Four of the lady senator's opponents in the Democratic primary were well-known, experienced party warriors. She was accorded no chance to win. But the Kingfish decided to demonstrate that he wielded influence outside his own state. He had a score to settle with Senator Joe Robinson. And Mrs. Caraway had voted for his resolution to limit incomes.

In late July, 1932, stacks of electioneering circulars were loaded into four Louisiana state-owned trucks and sent into Arkansas. One leaflet was entitled "Wall Street Versus The People"; another, "Why the Financiers Oppose Mrs. Caraway." Over more than 2,000 miles of Arkansas highway, Huey and Hattie led their truck caravan, meeting folks and speaking in thirty-nine county seats. The campaign trucks were equipped with records of popular music, amplifying horns, and a speaker's platform. When Long occupied the portable rostrum, a well-thumbed Bible lay on one side of him, an atomizer with throat spray on the other.

From Arkansas hamlets and road forks, voters crowded into the county seats to see and hear the Kingfish. His flying squads of huskies stood ready to eject an obstreperous drunk, quell fights, or soothe a crying baby. He would interrupt his denunciations of the rich to direct an aide to attend an infant so that the mother could listen to him. "Now I'm a-goin' to give you good ladies of Arkansas the benefit of what I've learned out of raisin' three children of my own," he would say, launching into a chat on baby care. "That's a good thing to know," he would conclude, "when you're not so fixed that you can hire nurses to take care of your children like the rich do." He would revert to his theme: "Herbert Hoover is callin' together boards and commissions. . . . What he needs to do is to read the Bible. The Lord tells us in Chapters 24, 26, and 27 of Leviticus, in Chapter 5 of Nehemiah and Chapter 5 of James . . . that unless you redistribute the wealth of a country into the hands of the people every fifty years, your country's got to go to ruination." He told the red-necked Arkansas farmers about their lady senator: "Why, she's got a better record in the Senate than even I have.... If Wall Street and their trust gang succeed in defeatin' enough Senators who have stood with the people like this little woman senator from Arkansas has, they'll have the whip hand on you."

"Miss Hattie's" six opponents, campaigning in the Southern tradition and equipped with frock coats and shoestring ties, were bewildered by this motorized combination of carnival and evangelism. In little more than one week of such stumping the Kingfish and the "Widder" won over enough rural Arkansans to return her to the Senate. The vote collected for her along the path of Long's sound-truck was greater than the combined total of her opponents.

During his tour for Mrs. Caraway, Long had boasted to Arkansans: "Back in my state of Louisiana, Mr. Broussard comes up for reelection. He's been one of Wall Street's own, and you just watch us clean that bird's plow." He proceeded to unseat Senator "Couzan Ed" Broussard and replace him with the supinely loyal Longite, John H. Overton, who had served as his counsel in the impeachment proceedings. At New Iberia Broussard appealed: "Long has been preaching a doctrine of division of wealth. When he comes here you ask him to divide with you"—and the Creole Senator told how Long lived in an $85,000 house and had arrived in Washington aboard a special railroad car. But most of the rural-parish voters were captivated by Huey's promises of redistribution of wealth. Overton was nominated in the primary.

At Broussard's demand, a United States Senate committee investigated the election. Long, as counsel for Overton, tangled with Samuel Tilden Ansel, counsel for the committee. When the committee chairman ordered Seymour Weiss, "treasurer" of Long's organization, to answer Ansel's question about the bank in which Overton's campaign funds were kept, Long interrupted: "I instruct him not to answer." Broussard's attorney, Edward Rightor, withdrew from the hearing on the grounds that the Louisiana public had lost confidence in the Senate committee. The committee declared that election practices unearthed in the Broussard-Overton primary were "a fraud upon the rights of citizens." Singularly enough, the Senate committee raised no question about Overton's right to take his Senate seat.

Controlling his own vote, as well as those of Mrs. Caraway and Overton, Long represented one thirty-second of the Senate membership. Except for the Majority Leader and the Minority Leader, he cast the most Senate votes.

VIII

Before taking his Senate seat in 1932, Long had filled the governor's chair, which he was vacating, with his ally, Alvin O. King, president pro tempore of the state senate. When his foe, Lieutenant Governor Paul N. Cyr, legally next to him in line, had himself sworn in as governor instead, Long threw a cordon of state troopers around the Executive Mansion and ordered Cyr arrested as an imposter. Long insisted that Cyr had vacated the Lieutenant Governor's office when he "illegally" attempted to take the gubernatorial oath. He received a court decision to this effect, then had King sworn in as lieutenant governor. King, not Cyr, finished Long's unexpired gubernatorial term.

Long entered a pact with Mayor T. Semmes Walmsley of New Orleans, chieftain of the "Old Regular" machine which he had previously denounced, in the campaign to elect his friend, Highway Chairman O. K. Allen, governor on a so-called "Complete the Work" ticket. Anti-Longites dubbed in the "Complete the Wreck" slate. Long stumped Louisiana for Allen. At Alexandria he denounced the New Orleans *Times-Picayune* as "low, lying, murderous and a bunch of skunks." His estranged brother, Julius T. Long, labeled Huey "the greatest political burglar of modern times." Kingfish's rural followers, with Walmsley's New Orleans machine, gave Allen victory. St. Bernard Parish, which in the senatorial primary of 1930 had given Long almost 4,000 votes to Ransdell's 9, now redeemed itself with a unanimous vote for Long's man Allen.

While in Washington, Long's thoughts were constantly on Louisiana. He made frequent trips home to check on his lieutenants and strengthen his control. As a federal senator he had no right on the floor of the legislature at Baton Rouge, but he regularly invaded formal sessions and committee meetings to issue orders on how members should vote. When a voice vote was called, he would sometimes reply. Often he occupied the Executive's chamber, forcing His Excellency to seek other quarters temporarily. In September 1932 Long told an audience in Opelousas: "You can charge me with anything Governor Allen has done." Once Julius Long declared: "No man with the resentment of a bird dog could take what Oscar took from Huey." Another Long brother, Earl, laughed: "A leaf blew in the window of Allen's office and fell on his desk. He signed it."

The situation in anti-Long New Orleans needed attention. Mayor Walmsley had finally shown independence and suspected that Long would engulf him and the entire metropolis. The Kingfish came to a parting of the ways with the mayor, issuing a pamphlet against the city's political ring, entitled "No Combination with Rats and Lice." But his candidate failed to defeat Walmsley for reelection.

Long set out to destroy Walmsley's power. In the summer of 1934 he intervened in the election of two congressmen from the New Orleans district. Armed with authority given him by a subservient judge, Long struck at the "Old Regulars" ' weakest spot, their lucrative practice of tolerating gambling and prostitution. Long announced that unless the "lottery kings, racketeering ward bosses, dives, and bawdy houses" were suppressed, he would "march into New Orleans." Walmsley shouted defiance. Governor Allen followed orders by declaring martial law in the city and dispatching steel-helmeted infantry, cavalry, and artillery companies of Louisiana national guardsmen. Troopers seized the office of the Registrar of Voters in order, so Long announced, "to prevent election frauds."

Mayor Walmsley exhorted President Roosevelt to enforce the United States constitutional provision that prohibits martial law in peacetime. But the off-year elections of 1934 were not far off; the President and his aides turned a deaf ear to the mayor's plea. Meanwhile, Long had himself charged with the investigation of vice in New Orleans. On Election Day 3,000 troops were ordered to sleep on their arms. Long's candidates for Congress won. From his Hotel Roosevelt suite, the Kingfish ruled as sovereign of the South's great seaport.

Long's sudden interest in "cleaning up" New Orleans provoked his brother Julius. The Baton Rouge *States-Times* of September 11, 1934, quoted Julius Long: "Huey was using a pretended investigation into vice conditions of New Orleans as a smokescreen for his nefarious efforts to further subject a free people.... With his well-known record for approving gambling and vice, fraud and ballot-box stuffing ... supported now by some of the outstanding gamblers and dive owners in and around New Orleans ... he has the audacity and little respect for the intelligence and liberties of the people to pretend that he sincerely wants to suppress vice and has called out the National Guard and state militia."

Certainly Huey Long was no reformer of vice and gambling. Early in 1935, six months after his "seizure" of New Orleans, he met Frank Costello, slot machine monarch of the nation's underworld, and arranged with Costello to install slot machines in the Louisiana metropolis. Later Costello testified before a New York grand jury that the Senator desired to set up a state relief fund, a project which Costello described as "some kind of ordinance for the poor, the blind . . . a certain kind of relief. . . ." The gambling and racketeering tycoon agreed with Long to pay into this project a certain sum for each slot machine in operation, although subsequently various factors reduced the charitable fund to a paltry $600 during the first year. The corporation "front" for the operation of the machines was a company with an innocent-sounding name. One of Costello's close associates was put in general charge of the racket and moved to New Orleans, together with several relatives who were employed as collectors. Long's interests were protected by one of the Senator's bodyguards. Shortly before Long's death, in 1935, the "company" began operations.

IX

After he had taken over New Orleans, Long gave attention to strengthening his rule throughout the entire state. On November 3, 1934, he forced his "trained seal" legislators to give him almost complete control over the vital activities of life in the state. In five days, almost like Hitler directing the Reichstag, or Stalin decreeing to the Congress of Soviets, the Kingfish had the legislature pass his personal laws—laws that stripped the courts of their power to curb Governor Allen in the use of the militia; that gave to the same marionette executive the control over primary and election machinery; that deprived cities, including New Orleans, of home rule; that set up a secret police force on the European totalitarian model, with the same powers in every community as the local police.

Effective as a weapon in Long's hands was his power to tax, a power used so effectively by Frank Hague in Jersey City. Taxation was a club with which to punish political foes. In a speech in Bienville Parish on September 1, 1932, the Kingfish boasted to his audience how he had used the "assessorial" power against John Ewing, publisher of the *Shreveport Times*. He chortled: "We put up the assessment of 'Squirt' Ewing 100 percent."

Important in keeping voters loyal to Long were his various public projects, achievements that seemed monumental in contrast to those of his predecessors. Besides providing free textbooks to every schoolchild, he built the Lake Pontchartrain seawall and the airport, which he named for a lieutenant, Abe Shushan; he constructed the Donner canal and levee at Algiers, across the Mississippi from New Orleans; he put up the medical center and other buildings of the Louisiana State University; he laid hundreds of miles of concrete roads; and he completed the skyscraper State Capitol at Baton Rouge. These improvements were thoroughly publicized in *Progress,* campaign leaflets, and stump speeches. Of the $5,000,000 worth of steel and stone that was the Capitol, Long gave his studied opinion: "Only one building compares with it for architecture. That's St. Peter's Cathedral in Rome, Italy."

Long's projects, of course, cost astronomically, for each contract let out by his regime had a surplus of graft tied to it. Back in 1932 Archie Burford, head of the United States Treasury agents in the southern territory, reported to his boss in Washington, Elmer L. Irey: "Chief, Louisiana is crawling. Long and his gang are stealing everything in the state . . . and they're not paying taxes on the loot." Thirty-two "T" agents were sent into the Pelican State to investigate, and soon Long was endeavoring to pressure the Hoover administration into calling them back. Insufficient evidence was collected for an indictment before Hoover turned over the presidency to Roosevelt early in 1933. Hoover's secretary of the treasury, Ogden L. Mills, bequeathed the case to his successor, William H. Woodin. "After all," said Mills to Irey, "the Senator is one of their [the Democrats'] babies; let them decide what to do with him." They did little, then. Early in 1934 Woodin's successor, Henry Morgenthau Jr. instructed Irey: "Get all your agents back on the Louisiana job. Start the investigation of Huey Long and proceed as though you were investigating John Doe. And let the chips fall where they may." By this year, Long had broken with the President and was nursing presidential ambitions of his own. Said Irey in retrospect: "We already knew that Long and his gang had collected millions of dollars in graft in the course of spending State loans that Huey had systematically raised to an even $100,000,000. Technically we were uninterested in graft payments but concerned only with the fact taxes had not been paid on these bribes."

By the end of 1934 Long and his court chamberlains had transformed their Louisiana bossdom into an almost full-blown dictatorship, with handsome financial profit to themselves. One of Long's top colleagues moved up from owner of a barbershop to owner of an expensive hotel.

Louisiana's dictator-demagogue prepared to challenge President Roosevelt.

X

In Huey Long's increasingly carping criticism of the President could be detected his own ambition to displace him in the White House. Roosevelt had hardly been inaugurated before he and Long developed sharp differences.

Long demanded Louisiana's share of federal jobs immediately. To preserve party harmony, Postmaster-

General Farley arranged a meeting between the President and Long in June 1933. The Senator charged into the White House angrily. He reminded the Chief Executive that he was largely responsible for his nomination at Chicago, a claim that surprised Roosevelt and Farley. He discussed federal jobs for Louisiana. Roosevelt remained unimpressed. When the meeting ended, Long growled to Farley: "What the hell is the use of coming down to see this fellow? I can't win any decisions over him."

Long's relations with the President became worse. When he was not permitted to name the officials to administer "make-work" federal projects, he was infuriated. He had laws passed by his puppet legislature virtually to take control of federal money expended in Louisiana out of the hands of the Roosevelt-appointed officials. He waxed indignant when Roosevelt heeded the recommendation of Mississippi Senator Pat Harrison in appointing the Collector of the Port of New Orleans.

Long's hankering for the White House became stronger. In August 1933 he went to New York to raise funds for his weekly, whose name he changed from the *Louisiana Progress* to the *American Progress* in keeping with his national ambitions. Before news reporters he called for more inflation "so's the people can be freed from debt." He thumbed open a Bible at Leviticus. "The Bible says you gotta free your people of debt every seven years," he began, and read that which the Lord spake unto Moses. He called for a capital levy tax.

Late in 1933 the Kingfish published his autobiography, *Every Man A King,* a medley of self-praise as the downtrodden's friend and an appeal for equalization of the nation's wealth. He released to the press a letter to the Washington *Social Register,* demanding that his name be deleted from that directory of the socially pedigreed. In February 1934 *American Progress* announced in red headlines: "Share Wealth Move Begun: People Will Set Up Local Organizations Throughout Nation." Long retained the evangelical anti-Semitic preacher from Shreveport, Reverend Gerald L. K. Smith, as organizer for a network of "Share-Our-Wealth" clubs throughout the United States. Long's movement spread up to the depression-ravaged industrial Northeast and into the then poor farm states of the Middle West and Far West. "Next to me," confided Long to one lieutenant, "Gerald Smith is the greatest rabble-rouser in the country."

The same lieutenant later revealed that the Kingfish intended to use the clubs, instead of the Roosevelt-dominated Democratic party, as a vehicle on which to ride to the White House. In 1936 Long planned to run as an independent candidate against Roosevelt and the Republican candidate. He thought he could carry Louisiana, a few other southern states such as Arkansas, Mississippi, and Alabama, and maybe drought-stricken Oklahoma and North Dakota, thus taking enough electoral votes from Roosevelt to enable the Republican candidate to be elected. This would discredit Roosevelt and Long could then run against the Republican President in 1940. The national Democratic Party might be destroyed in the process but Long considered his own election more important. (In the same way, Senator Joseph R. McCarthy of Wisconsin was to place his own career above the welfare of the Republican Party in the 1950's.)

The "Share-Our-Wealth" clubs multiplied mushroom-like throughout the South, the border regions, and parts of the North. Their success, plus Long's harangues on the Senate floor and over the radio, alarmed Roosevelt and his advisers. Postmaster-General Farley, still chairman of the Democratic National Committee, had his staff conduct a nationwide secret poll to ascertain if the Louisiana demagogue's ideas were attracting many potential voters. To the distress of the Democratic Party high command, the poll indicated that Long, on a third-party ticket, might poll between 3,000,000 and 4,000,000 votes for the presidency. Farley also received the frightening news that certain wealthy conservatives, in their strong disapproval of Roosevelt and the New Deal, and their desire to defeat the Democratic Party, might finance a Long-for-President campaign in 1936. Said Farley in his book, *Behind the Ballots:* "He [Long] was head and shoulders stronger than any of the other 'Messiahs' who were also gazing wistfully at the White House and wondering what chance they would have to arrive there as the result of a popular uprising. It was easy to conceive of a situation whereby Long, by polling more than 3,000,000 votes, might have the balance of power in the 1936 election."

The Roosevelt administration's fight to destroy Long took two forms: a counter-campaign on the radio against him, and an acceleration of the move to put him in jail for income-tax evasion.

Roosevelt's forces selected General Hugh Johnson, former National Recovery Administrator, to spear the Kingfish over the airwaves with his sharp tongue. On the radio in March 1935, Johnson blisteringly assailed Long and the demagogue-priest, Father Charles E. Coughlin, as "Pied-Pipers" and deluders of the people. The General barked into the microphone: "Hitler couldn't hold a candle to Huey in the art of the old Barnum ballyhoo—a new sucker born every second." Long demanded and received a nationwide hook-up to answer Johnson. Millions, who tuned in and heard the Senator appeal to them to telephone their friends and tell them that he was on the air, expected him to answer Johnson, epithet for epithet. Instead, Long dismissed the General as Roosevelt's "lately lamented pampered ex-Crown Prince" and spoke on the maldistribution of wealth, with barbed thrusts at the President. A home, an automobile, a radio, and $2,000 yearly for every family; a free college education for all; a $4,000,000 limitation on individual fortunes—these were his promises. He was vague about how he would make this roseate picture a reality, but membership in the "Share-Our-Wealth" clubs soared.

In the same year, 1935, Long sang over a New Orleans radio station his presidential campaign song, "Every Man a King":

(Verse)
Why sleep or slumber, America?
    Land of brave and true;
With castles, clothing, and food for all,
    All belongs to you.

(Chorus)
Every man a king; every man a king;
    For you can be a millionaire.
But there's something belonging to others,
    There's enough for all people to share.
When it's sunny June or December too,
    Or in the wintertime or spring,
There'll be peace without end,
Every neighbor a friend,
    With every man a king.

Meanwhile, Chief Irey and his agents, after months of undercover investigation, had found evidence that nearly every contract let out by the Louisiana state administration had been graft-ridden, and no income taxes paid on the graft. Former Governor Dan Moody of Texas was picked to prosecute Long and his associates. The "T-Men" succeeded in having one

Long lieutenant, State Representative Joseph Fisher, indicted for not paying federal income taxes on "commissions" he had received on state highway projects. Fisher was found guilty and sentenced to eighteen months in the Atlanta penitentiary. The next Longite on the list was Abe Shushan, President of the New Orleans Levee Board.

At a conference with Moody on September 7, the Treasury agents discussed the case against Long, which would be based on evasion of income taxes on graft that he had received. They would "get" him in connection with the "Win or Lose Corporation," in which he held 31 shares. Moody assured Irey: "I will go before the grand jury when it meets next month and ask for an indictment against Long."

On the following day—September 8, 1935—Long was shot.

XI

Long personified the dictatorship threat in America. Louisiana under his whip was a monocracy, a government by unilateral control, with no room for legislative or judicial checks. Long hated the press and commanded bodyguards to give reporters the "rush." He said: "I'm the Constitution around here!" He snapped his fingers and his top-heavy majority in the legislature voted as he directed. He gave orders to judges, and they rendered court decisions upholding his actions. His dominance of the militia, the election officials, and the tax-assessing bodies, through his puppet Governor, left citizens no redress, either through electoral or legislative action.

In his use of military force, distribution of patronage, destruction of local government, and hamstringing of normal parliamentary procedures, the Kingfish suggested Adolf Hitler, Benito Mussolini, Joseph Stalin, and Juan Domingo Perón. His legislature numbered almost as many robots proportionately as did Der Führer's Reichstag, Il Duce's Chamber of Deputies, the Red Premier's "People's" parliament, or the Argentinian Colonel's Congress. Long's over the masses and use of secret police were similar to theirs.

Like almost all dictators, Long constantly feared for his personal safety. In July 1935, on the Senate floor, he announced that a plot to assassinate him had been uncovered. His informers had assured him that opponents, meeting in a New Orleans hotel room, had talked of "one man, one gun, one bullet," and asked each other: "Does anyone doubt that President Roosevelt would pardon the man who rid the country of Huey Long?" For weeks Long talked of violent and sudden death. "Sure, I carry a gun. Sometimes I carry four. Can't tell when somebody's a-goin' to shoot the king." He spoke jocularly, but a grave look could be detected. Assassination was a persistent fear in Long's mind. He had ruined the careers of numerous men, who might attempt to retaliate. There were said to be those among his bodyguards who resented his harsh, sadistic overlordship. Countless vows of vengeance had been hurled at him in his climb to the Louisiana throne. The Kingfish surrounded himself with an increased number of armed bodyguards.

In August 1935, after arranging for publication of his second book, *My First Days in the White House,* the jittery Long decided that his Louisiana control was not yet complete. He ordered Governor Allen to call a special session of the legislature for early September. Among the unfinished business was curbing the political power of his long-time foe, Judge Benjamin F. Pavy of Opelousas.

Judge Pavy, of the judicial district that included the parishes of St. Landry and Evangeline, ruled as political leader jointly with District Attorney R. Lee Garland. Pavy climaxed a long feud in September 1932, when he denounced "election thievery" and sentenced five pro-Long election officials to a ten-day sojourn in jail for violation of an injunction against "dummy" candidates. The five Longites were pardoned by Governor Allen after two hours. A few days later, Long addressed an audience in Opelousas: "You may not have the judge and district attorney in St. Landry parish that I want, but that makes no difference to me. I will work for the people of St. Landry parish." Subsequently, Long accused Pavy of being part Negro.

Since the anti-Long parish of St. Landry and the pro-Long parish of Evangeline were yoked in the same judicial district, and since St. Landry outvoted

Evangeline, there was no way for the Kingfish to defeat the Pavy-Garland forces in an election. Accordingly, Long decided to "gerrymander" the judge and the district attorney out of power by act of his subservient legislature. Among the numerous Long-dictated bills introduced at the special session, which convened in September, was House Bill No. 1. That measure set off Evangeline Parish in a separate judicial district, and lumped St. Landry Parish in with the pro-Long parishes of Acadia, Lafayette, and Vermillion. The new district thus formed would, of course, be overwhelmingly pro-Long, and Pavy and Garland were due for a defeat when they came up for reelection.

Judge Pavy's family, friends, and political supporters waxed indignant over Long's plan. Pavy's son-in-law, Dr. Carl A. Weiss Jr., a Baton Rouge physician, was particularly incensed at the Kingfish's implication that there was Negro blood in the family. Long, undeterred by this opposition, went through with plans to have the bill enacted.

On Sunday night, September 8, 1935, in his skyscraper Capitol in Baton Rouge, Long ended a meeting of legislative leaders and lieutenants. He strutted along the marble hallway toward the office of Governor Allen, accompanied by Supreme Court Justice John B. Fournet, his bodyguards Joe Messina and Murphy Roden, and others. He paused to speak to henchmen. Suddenly a slight, bespectacled man in white suit—later identified as Dr. Weiss—stepped from behind a pillar opposite the Governor's office and approached Long. A shot rang out. Long tottered.

Whether the bullet came from Weiss's gun or from the guns of Long's bodyguards is still a matter of speculation in New Orleans and Baton Rouge. There is some evidence that the young doctor was not the assassin. He may have only intended to appeal for justice to Judge Pavy. At any rate the fatal bullet seems to have disappeared. Long staggered, wounded, his hand to his side. The bodyguards pumped a hail of bullets into Dr. Weiss. The young physician fell dead.

The wounded Kingfish struggled for his life in Our Lady of the Lake Hospital in Baton Rouge. Lieutenant Governor James A. Noe gave him a blood transfusion. Long was conscious during the first hours, except for the period of rest produced by administered narcotics. In periods of wakefulness, he allegedly mumbled: "Oh, Lord, don't let me die for I have a few more things to accomplish." Long died on September 10.

American Progress mourned the "passing of the man who will be known in the histories of tomorrow as 'the President who was assassinated before he was elected.'" The demagogue-priest, Father Charles E. Coughlin, termed Long's death "the most regrettable thing in modern history." Long's lieutenants—except those who ghoulishly looked to the succession—were grief-stricken.

Never had Baton Rouge witnessed crowds like

those that poured into the capital city to bid farewell to the Kingfish. Eighty thousand filed past his flower-banked bier as he lay in state in the Capitol, the scene of his greatest triumphs as well as his downfall. Highways on both sides of the Mississippi River were clogged with sorrowing people, afoot and in dilapidated cars.

When the funeral day came, 125,000 men, women and children massed about the Capitol under a broiling Louisiana sun. Some perched on rooftops and in oak trees hung with Spanish moss.

Reverend Gerald L. K. Smith, organizer of the Share-Our-Wealth clubs, preached the funeral sermon. "Greater love hath no man than this, that a man lay down his life for his friends," he began. A "statesman," a "tender father," a "musical heart that loved the songs of the common people"—Long had been all of them. "This blood which dropped upon this soil shall seal our hearts together. Take up the torch, complete the task. . . . His final prayer was this: 'Oh, God, don't let me die. I have a few more things to do.'"

Governor Allen, Lieutenant Governor Noe, Speaker of the House Allen Ellender, Justice Fournet, Robert Maestri, Seymour Weiss, Abe Shushan—richly-rewarded court chamberlains—marched as pallbearers.

The Kingfish was lowered into the grave in the sunken garden outside the Capitol. The assembled crowds wept. A hush fell, broken only by a soft dirge composed of "Nearer My God To Thee," "The Star Spangled Banner," and, in a minor key, "Every Man a King."

XII

Huey Long became the symbol of American demagoguery. Two movies and several novels, based on his life, have warned the country of the dangers of native dictatorship. Like other demagogues, he professed to be of and for the people. He was one of the "poor whites" of Louisiana who were struggling to emerge from the morass of semi-feudal existence. And because he was one of them, his followers thought he was for them. He built schools and hospitals, and then showed his scorn for education and health by using patronage to staff them. He talked of making every man a king and instead made them vassals. He brought scandal and corruption to his state and made a mockery of the American ideal of democracy. It was power he wanted and he did not care how many he crushed along the way. The poor of Louisiana's hills and canebrakes needed help and they trusted the Kingfish. Could they have guessed their hero was laughing at them, that his concern was for himself alone? Some demagogues go down to defeat at the polls, relegated to obscurity by a people grown weary of their broken promises, their corrupt practices, their real contempt. But other demagogues are struck down in anger in the final defeat of death.

No one can condone assassination, the rejection of law, the return to the primitive society of violence. Democracy can take care of its demagogues in its own way. But the death of Huey Long is a warning, nonetheless, that demagoguery breeds its own destruction. Dictatorship can bring revolt if men are tried too far. The pity was that Huey Long did not live so that Louisiana could have had the honor of voting him out of office.

About the Author

Historian Reinhard H. Luthin (1905–1962) was a frequent contributor to *The American Scholar, The American Historical Review, The Political Science Quarterly* and other journals. A former fellow in history at Duke University and former member of the history faculty at Columbia University, he was Fulbright Professor of American and European history at the University of Dacca, Pakistan, and a visiting lecturer at Trinity College, Hartford, Connecticut. Other works include *The Real Abraham Lincoln* and *The First Lincoln Campaign.*

Printed in Great Britain
by Amazon